No matter how you feel, get up. Dress up. Show up & NEVER give up.

Other Resources by
Pastor Rhonda Spencer

No! MORE HURT

PASTOR RHONDA SPENCER

Her life-changing book
NO MORE HURT
and accompanying workbook
are available at:
www.RhondaJSpencer.com
and
amazon.com

Living a WOW Life: 31 Day Devotional
is printed by CreateSpace
(an Amazon.com company)
and is available at amazon.com
and other retail outlets.

Remember who your actual enemy is...he's the originator of blame shifting. YOUR FIGHT IS NEVER AGAINST ANOTHER HUMAN BEING, it's against the enemy of your soul. He's seeking whom he may devour, 24/7. Put down your weapon against your brother, sister, spouse, co-worker, neighbor, etc. That's not the real source of your fight. **light bulb moment** That is why FORGIVENESS is so important; it lets you off the enemy's hook. He's winning as long as we have angst against another human being!!! People make mistakes but it's really the enemy out to destroy us. STAND FIRM AGAINST THE ENEMY OF YOUR SOUL and STOP fighting EACH OTHER. We are all on the same human team against the devil, who wants to take us out with him. As long as we are fighting against flesh and blood we are joining the wrong team, the losing team.

"For we are not fighting against flesh-and-blood enemies, but against evil rulers and authorities of the unseen world, against mighty powers in this dark world, and against evil spirits in the heavenly places." Ephesians 6:12

Never take up a fight against another person (especially your spouse). They are not the real enemy or source. Our fight, stress and turmoil is never with people. There is an enemy of your soul that is seeking to steal, kill, destroy, discourage and divide you, and he is on task, 24/7.

Do not let what people say and do cause you hurt, offense or bitterness because it is not people that we wrestle against; it is the enemy of our soul, the unseen forces, that we war against. So direct your war against those forces, not ever against a human being, a person--your struggle is never with a person. So take every offense, hurt and discouragement off that person that you thought it was against.

YOU ARE NOT ALONE. The King of kings stands with you and His angelic forces encamp around you.

You are safely placed on solid rock.
Your heart, mind and life are protected from any harm.
Sometimes we can feel outnumbered.
THERE ARE MORE FOR YOU THAN AGAINST YOU!!!

"Don't be afraid!" Elisha told him. "For there are more on our side than on theirs!" Then Elisha prayed, "O Lord, open his eyes and let him see!" The Lord opened the young man's eyes, and when he looked up, he saw that the hillside around Elisha was filled with horses and chariots of fire.   2 Kings 6:16-17 NLT

Whether you can see them or not, the angelic forces surround you and you are not outnumbered.

You are deeply loved.
God is pursuing you endlessly; yes you.
You are going to get through this
BECAUSE HE IS WITH YOU.
Hold your head up.
Silence the doubt on your tongue.
Smile the fear off your face.
You are on solid rock.
You can not fail BECAUSE HE IS WITH YOU.
Laugh at any attempts to stop you.
No person, no past, no bondage, no addiction...nothing is
greater than the ALL POWERFUL.
He has got you covered.

Enjoy this day that the Lord has made, He walks in it
before you, surrounds you, and is even your rear guard.

For [although] they hold a form of true religion, they deny and reject and are strangers TO THE POWER OF IT [their conduct belies the genuineness of their profession]. Avoid [all] such people [turn away from them]. 2 Timothy 3:5

There is NOTHING IMPOSSIBLE for our ALL POWERFUL God!!!! Does our conduct reflect the genuineness of that profession? If actions speak louder than words, what are we saying? Are we strangers to the power of God? There are times when our intentions and our actions don't line up. We would never intend to deny God's power but when we let words of fear, stress, worry and defeat come out, that is what we are doing. We can be strangers to the power of God without even knowing it! Let's let our actions line up with our hearts' intentions.

GOD'S WORD IS TRUE and nothing is impossible. Base every action and thought on this truth today! Let your actions speak that you believe.

Victories will be won today.

I pray that your hearts will be flooded with light so that you can understand the <u>confident hope</u> He has given to those He called-that you can know and understand what is the IMMEASURABLE, UNLIMITED AND SURPASSING GREATNESS OF HIS POWER IN AND FOR US who believe, as demonstrated in the working of His mighty strength, this is the same mighty power that raised Christ from the dead and seated Him in the place of honor at God's right hand in the heavenly realms. Ephesians 1:18-20

YOU HAVE POWER THAT IS IMMEASURABLE, UNLIMITED AND SURPASSING WORKING IN YOU!!! His power working in and through you is stronger than anything that threatens you.

I pray that this truth is revealed to you today and that you will be flooded with light so you can understand the power you have is immeasurable, unlimited and SURPASSING.

Surpassing! That's like in a race when a runner blows past another runner, **the power in you blows past anything that threatens you.**

I want you to think of that thing that you feel is threatening you and I want you to see the power of God surpass it.

NO THING is more powerful than God inside of you.

Day 7

You are Safe and Secure.

Psalm 17:8 Keep me as the apple of Your eye; hide me under the shadow of Your wings.

Psalm 23:4 Yea, though I walk through the valley of the shadow of death, I will fear no evil; For You are with me.

Psalm 91:11 For He will command His angels concerning you to guard you in all your ways.

Psalm 40:2 He also brought me up out of a horrible pit, out of the miry clay, and set my feet upon a rock, and established my steps.

Isaiah 58:8 The glory of the LORD shall be your rear guard

Isaiah 52:12 For the LORD will go before you...

2 Samuel 22:37 You enlarged my path under me; so my feet did not slip.

Job 33:11 He watches all my paths.

Jeremiah 29:11 "For I know the plans I have for you," declares the LORD, "plans to prosper you and not to harm you, plans to give you hope and a future.

Luke 10:19 Behold, I give you the authority to trample on serpents and scorpions, and over all the power of the enemy, and nothing shall by any means hurt you.

John 14:27 Peace I leave with you; My [own] peace I now give and bequeath to you. Not as the world gives do I give to you. Do not let your hearts be troubled, neither let them be afraid. [Stop allowing yourselves to be agitated and disturbed; and do not permit yourselves to be fearful and intimidated and cowardly and unsettled.]

Day 8

"You are blessed because you believed that the Lord would do what he said." Luke 1:45

Even when there was no reason for hope, Abraham kept hoping. Romans 4:18

Abraham never wavered in believing God's promise. <u>In fact, his faith grew stronger</u>, and in this he brought glory to God. He was fully convinced that God is able to do whatever he promises." Romans 4:20-21

NEVER GIVE UP!!!! 💕 GOD IS ABLE!!!

"I will answer them before they even call to me. While they are still talking about their needs, I will go ahead and answer their prayers!"

Isaiah 65:24

Luke 10:19 says NOTHING has the power to hurt you.

Pain is common in this world but pain becomes
hurt when it's allowed to do damage.

Don't pay pain any attention.

If you hear somebody is talking about you, pay no
attention. Give it no energy. It's a distraction from the
plans for your life. Instead of getting upset with them,
remember, people don't talk about ordinary people; they
talk about exceptional people. Take it as a compliment
and never change the love you have for them or for
imperfect people.

Ecclesiastes 7:21 says, "Don't eavesdrop on others-you may
hear your servant curse you."

God, I pray that no pain she experiences can get to the
place of hurt in her life or mind. I pray that her love will
remain like yours, unconditional; and that she will
NEVER HURT AGAIN.

Pay it no attention at all, you are perfectly loved by the
Master, the King, the Creator. Knowing His love takes
away every ounce of fear.

Have a loved, free-from-hurt day.

It's not a
competition
AGAINST
each other,
the goal is
for everyone
to make it!
2 Peter 3:9

It is God's desire that everyone makes it and that
no one will perish; and that includes the people
you don't like. Refuse to compete against anyone,
God thinks we are all to die for.

Romans 12:15 Rejoice with those who rejoice;
weep with those who weep.
1 Thessalonians 5:11 So encourage each other and
build each other up.
Hebrews 3:13 But encourage one another daily.

Don't just cross the finish line alone; take as many
people with you as you can. It's not a competition
in which only one wins, so refuse to compete
against others.

Here's some power for advancement;
no need to cower or curl up in a ball...
move forward with your Shield of Faith up.

I DECREE AND I DECLARE!

In the Name of Jesus, we cancel every satanic assignment against us, our family, our business and our church. We cancel every assignment sent to steal from us, kill and destroy us.

We close every door or crack giving access to our minds, our families, our property, our finances and our current and future opportunities.

We speak that every operation that has been at work against us must be stopped, in Jesus name.
Every interference working in our lives is evicted right now, they must halt immediately.

We put a stop order on every written form of assignment that has been published against us and that they, now, are made of no effect. Silence very voice raised up to accuse us.

We release angelic forces to work on our behalf, clearing the way before us.

In the Name of Jesus, we declare that every weapon formed against us will not prosper.

Have a victorious day.

Day 12

"What's the price of a pet canary? Some loose change, right? And God cares what happens to it even more than you do. He pays even greater attention to you, down to the last detail—even numbering the hairs on your head! So don't be intimidated by all this bully talk. You're worth more than a million canaries." Matthew 10:29-31

"Keep me as the apple of Your eye; hide me under the shadow of Your wings," Psalms 17:8

Do you feel unimportant? Insignificant? Overlooked? Invisible? You are PERFECTLY loved and important to the One who matters most .

🩶 His focus is you and every detail of your life. Not one hair of your head falls without Him noticing.

You are the apple of God's eye. That means you're the center of His attention all day, every day.

Day 3

ASK GOD! "You haven't asked Me."

"Keep on asking, and you will receive what you ask for.
Keep on seeking, and you will find. Keep on knocking,
and the door will be opened to you. For everyone who
asks, receives. Everyone who seeks, finds. And to
everyone who knocks, the door will be opened. You
parents—if your children ask for a loaf of bread, do you
give them a stone instead? Or if they ask for a fish, do you
give them a snake? Of course not! So if you sinful people
know how to give good gifts to your children, how much
more will your heavenly Father give good gifts to those
who ask him." Matthew 7:7-11

Ahhhh the Word of God!!!!!
I BELIEVE WITHOUT DOUBT.
My Father NEVER disappoints. (Romans 5:5)

A widow of that city came to him repeatedly, saying,
"Give me justice in this dispute with my enemy."
The judge ignored her for a while, but finally he said to
himself, "I don't fear God or care about people, but this
woman is driving me crazy. I'm going to see that she gets
justice, because she is wearing me out with her constant
requests!" Then the Lord said, "Learn a lesson from this
unjust judge. Even he rendered a just decision in the end.
So don't you think God will surely give justice to his
chosen people who cry out to him day and night? Will he
keep putting them off? I tell you, he will grant justice to
them quickly!" Luke 18:3-8

When was the last time you asked God about it? ASK.

💜 I'm hearing it loud and clear from Daddy, ASK,
SEEK, KNOCK---you'll receive, find and it'll be opened.

Look at the Birds and the Lilies they don't worry about a thing, your Father takes care of them...HOW MUCH MORE WILL HE TAKE CARE OF YOU (every single detail you can trust God to work out).

"Therefore I tell you, stop being perpetually uneasy (anxious and worried) about your life, what you shall eat or what you shall drink; or about your body, what you shall put on. Is not life greater [in quality] than food, and the body [far above and more excellent] than clothing? Look at the birds of the air; they neither sow nor reap nor gather into barns, and yet your heavenly Father keeps feeding them. Are you not worth much more than they? And who of you by worrying and being anxious can add one unit of measure (cubit) to his stature or to the span of his life? And why should you be anxious about clothes? Consider the lilies of the field and learn thoroughly how they grow; they neither toil nor spin. Yet I tell you, even Solomon in all his magnificence (excellence, dignity, and grace) was not arrayed like one of these. But if God so clothes the grass of the field, which today is alive and green and tomorrow is tossed into the furnace, will He not much more surely clothe you, O you of little faith? Therefore do not worry and be anxious, saying, What are we going to have to eat? or, What are we going to have to drink? or, What are we going to have to wear? For the Gentiles (heathen) wish for and crave and diligently seek all these things, and your heavenly Father knows well that you need them all. But seek (aim at and strive after) first of all His kingdom and His righteousness (His way of doing and being right), and then all these things taken together will be given you besides."   Matthew 6:25-33

Day 14

GO CARE-FREE TODAY.
"What a God! You protect me with salvation-armor;
You hold me up with a firm hand. You cleared the ground
under me so my footing was firm. His road stretches
straight and smooth. Every God-direction is road-tested.
Everyone who runs toward Him makes it." Psalm 18:30-42

Keep going Woman of God; you're going to make it.
God has already cleared the ground for your next step
and the road is pretested.

You are equipped and anointed for this road.

Let EVERY fear, stress, pain and anxiety go to Him.
You're going to BREAKTHROUGH not breakdown.

*He will cover
you with his
feathers.
He will shelter
you with his
wings.
His faithful
promises are
your armor
and
protection.*
Psalms 91:4

The torrents will flow, the winds may pound upon you but you will not collapse. You are on Solid Rock. You are still standing and will remain standing. It's NOT your strength, it's the power of the ALMIGHTY God in you. You will not be shaken.
You will remain STABLE and FIXED.

"HE WHO dwells in the secret place of the Most High shall remain stable and fixed." Psalm 91:1

"God, the one and only - everything I need comes from Him. He's solid rock under my feet, breathing room for my soul, an impregnable castle: I'm set for life."
Psalm 62:1-2

"Rest in God alone, my soul, for my hope comes from Him. He alone is my rock and my salvation, my stronghold; I will not be shaken. My salvation and glory depend on God, my strong rock. My refuge is in God. Trust in Him at all times, you people; pour out your hearts before Him. God is our refuge. Selah"
Psalms 62:5-8

""Therefore, everyone who hears these words of Mine and acts on them will be like a sensible man who built his house on the rock. The rain fell, the rivers rose, and the winds blew and pounded that house. Yet it didn't collapse, because its foundation was on the rock."
Matthew 7:24-25

You will not collapse,
you have solid rock under your feet.

BE THE DIFFERENCE.

If you think there isn't enough love in the world, be love.
If you want your spouse to treat you like you're of great importance to him, treat him like he is of great importance.

If you think people aren't friendly, be friendly.
If you think the Holy Spirit isn't moving in the church, allow the Holy Spirit to move mightily in you.

You can't change others but you can change YOU and that will then change the world, one person at a time.
IF YOU WANT TO SEE A DIFFERENCE,
BE THE DIFFERENCE!!!

"Don't copy the behavior and customs of this world, but let God transform you into a new person by changing the way you think. Then you will learn to know God's will for you, which is good and pleasing and perfect."
Romans 12:2

Life will be different if you are different; otherwise we are just in another day and another year will go by.

BE THE DIFFERENCE

Day 17

Don't fall to this trap of the enemy. Too many women have already fallen to it. If you look around it's almost epidemic!!! PLEASE SOUND THE ALARM TO THE WOMEN AROUND YOU.

Ladies! I wanted to extend an urgent warning! Whatever you don't guard, the enemy will come in and plunder. The Word tells us to "Be alert and of sober mind. Your enemy the devil prowls around like a roaring lion looking for someone to devour. Resist him, standing firm in the faith, because you know that the family of believers throughout the world is undergoing the same kind of sufferings." 1 Peter 5:8-9

There is a demonic assignment against marriages! At this moment the enemy is looking for a foothold in our relationships. Do not trust any thought, situation, or reasoning that might put you or any other wife against her husband! Marriage is meant to reflect the intimacy and relationship of Jesus with the church! Marriage unites two people in vision, action, and faith! If the enemy can create division in our marriage then he can divide, disarm, and dilute the power of our marriage, the power of the gospel! Keep your eyes open, stay aware, warn others! Encourage one another to uplift, pray for, and fiercely protect their husbands! Only the Word of God can be trusted! "Whatever God has joined together let NO man (or woman) put asunder." Mark 10:9

Dry?.......

"Though its roots have grown old in the earth and its stump decays, at the scent of water it will bud and sprout again like a new seedling." Job 14:8-9

Often a tree is used as symbolic of a righteous man. Job was saying that there is always hope for a righteous man and that though he may fall down from time to time, he will always rise again.

For a righteous man may fall seven times and rise again. Proverbs 24:16

Job goes on to say that regardless of how dire it gets for the righteous, describing the situation "as having old roots" and a dead stump, at the scent of water, new life will spring forth. So no matter how spiritually dead one might become, he or she can be revived by the scent of water.
What is this water?
It is the living water, the Word of God.

...that He might sanctify and cleanse her with the washing of water by the word, Ephesians 5:26

The Word of God truly is Spirit and life. It has the power to revive those who have died spiritually. You don't even need a gulp of it; a scent or merely a whiff is enough! The fragrance of the Word brings life into any dry, dead or stench-filled situation. The devil came to bring death and destruction but Jesus came that we may have life and have it abundantly.

DRY...

For the Word that God speaks is alive and full of power [making it active, operative, energizing, and effective]; it is sharper than any two-edged sword, penetrating to the dividing line of the breath of life (soul) and [the immortal] spirit, and of joints and marrow [of the deepest parts of our nature], exposing and sifting and analyzing and judging the very thoughts and purposes of the heart. Hebrews 4:12

A scent of the active, operative, energizing and effective Word of God is enough to give hope to any seemingly dead situation and revive you. Don't give up.
Just sniff the water!

"For I am like a tree whose roots reach the water, whose branches are refreshed with the dew." Job 29:19

"But his delight is in the law of the LORD, and in His law he meditates day and night. He shall be like a tree planted by the rivers of water, that brings forth its fruit in its season, whose leaf also shall not wither; and whatever he does shall prosper." Psalms 1:2-3

"Thus says the LORD: 'Cursed is the man who trusts in man and makes flesh his strength, whose heart departs from the LORD. For he shall be like a shrub in the desert, and shall not see when good comes, but shall inhabit the parched places in the wilderness, in a salt land which is not inhabited. Blessed is the man who trusts in the LORD, and whose hope is the LORD. For he shall be like a tree planted by the waters, which spreads out its roots by the river, and will not fear when heat comes; but its leaf will be green, and will not be anxious in the year of drought, nor will cease from yielding fruit.'" Jeremiah 17:5-8

A whiff of His Word is more than enough to transform your atmosphere, your outlook, YOUR LIFE.

Day 20

Pray in the Holy Spirit today and wash your mind with rivers of water. It will refresh you, renew you and bring joy.

"Pray in the power of the Holy Spirit. In this way, you will keep yourselves safe in God's love. Now all glory to God, who is able to KEEP YOU FROM FALLING AWAY and will bring you with great joy into His glorious presence without a single fault." Jude 1:20-21, 24

When you pray in the Holy Spirit there is JOY and PEACE...if you have no joy or peace, PRAY IN THE SPIRIT UNTIL YOU ARE FULL. I am convinced this is why Paul said, "I pray in the spirit more than you all." He needed it. I need it, you need it. It's the promise of the Father. He desires you to have abundant life of joy and peace so let's water the empty and dry places and get full of joy.

"For the kingdom of God is not eating and drinking, but righteousness and peace and joy in the Holy Spirit." Romans 14:17

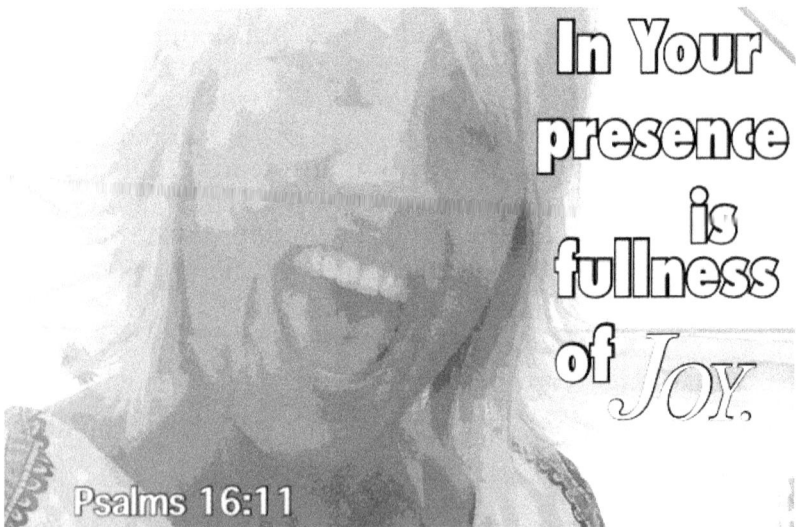

In Your presence is fullness of Joy.

Psalms 16:11

Runners in a race do not look back because it slows them down; it can even cause them to trip and fall and be taken out of the race. If you are focusing on the past...that thing that happened...or what they said...that rejection...that abandonment...that mistake...that very painful situation...

IT'S HOLDING YOU BACK.

We reap what we sow. If we spend time thinking on those things; we are sowing seeds of that into our current lives, and now it's become the prophecy of our future.

So forget those things which are behind. Yes, just simply let them go. By having your hook in them, you're only hurting yourself and your race to win.

"I don't mean to say that I have already achieved these things or that I have already reached perfection. But I press on to possess that perfection for which Christ Jesus first possessed me. No, dear brothers and sisters, I have not achieved it, but I focus on this one thing: Forgetting the past and looking forward to what lies ahead, I press on to reach the end of the race and receive the heavenly prize for which God, through Christ Jesus, is calling us." Philippians 3:12-14

You weren't born at a different time or a different place or with different circumstances. You were born you, perfectly you, designed for where you're at and with the call of God. So forget about "if things were just different I could do this," and press on to win the race. Take off all those heavy loads and run with freedom.

What little thing or even major thing from your past comes up in your mind? Choose to forget it and let it go...PRESS ON MY BEAUTIFUL FRIEND.

"I will go before you and level the mountains [to make the crooked places straight]; I will break in pieces the doors of bronze and cut asunder the bars of iron. And I will give you the treasures of darkness and hidden riches of secret places, that you may know that it is I, the Lord God, Who calls you by your name." Isaiah 45:2-3

Are you facing a mountain? No problem.
Does the way in front of you seems crooked? No problem.
Are you coming up to closed doors? No problem.

He levels your mountains and makes the crooked path straight. He will break in pieces those closed doors. Why? So that you will know that He is YOUR God and He knows who you are.

Day 23

This is me holding your face in my hands, speaking to you this morning:

You ARE on SOLID rock and not on sinking sand.
You have NEVER lived an alone moment in your life.
GOD IS WITH YOU.
You are accepted, loved and treasured.

There is nothing, NOTHING that by ANY means can hurt you. You have hope and a future. You are NOT going to breakdown, you're going to BREAKTHROUGH!

The all mighty power of God is MORE THAN enough for you. It's stronger than ANYTHING and EVERYTHING you'll EVER face.

"Fear not, for I have redeemed you; I have called you by your name; You are Mine. When you pass through the waters, I will be with you; and through the rivers, they shall not overflow you. When you walk through the fire, you shall not be burned, nor shall the flame scorch you. For I am the LORD your God. Isaiah 43:1-3

Knowing (God's) PERFECT LOVE for you casts out all fear 🤍 1 John 4:18

LIVE FEARLESS.

I was called an extremist. My response was, "I don't do anything halfway."

If we stop to ask ourselves this question:
How would I do it if I were doing it for Jesus?
(Because that is exactly how we're supposed to do everything, as if we were doing unto the Lord.) I think it would change how we do a lot of things in our day-to-day lives if we looked at it as if we were doing it unto the Lord.

"Whatever may be your task, work at it heartily (from the soul), as [something done] for the Lord and not for men," Colossians 3:23

"If you are faithful in little things, you will be faithful in large ones. Luke 16:10

No matter what your task is, do it your best. If all you have is a t-shirt to clean; wash it, press it and hang it. If your job is to clean the toilets; scrub them inside and out and put air fresheners in them. Whatever your task, menial or very important, do your best and do it for God.

Day 25

All scripture is profitable... 2 Tim 3:16

Saturate yourself with the Word. It is God, it's the power of God. The Word is supernatural, it is the literal presence of God!!! Whatever you are going through, whether you're on the mountain top or in a dark valley, the Word will strengthen you, give you the power to do the impossible and sow seeds of the supernatural in your life. When you are daily sowing the supernatural you can EXPECT THE SUPERNATURAL daily...miracles, signs, wonders, favor, health and the impossible WILL BE YOUR PORTION.

So shall my word be that goes out from my mouth; it shall not return to me empty, but it shall accomplish that which I purpose, and shall succeed in the thing for which I sent it. Isaiah 55:11

Love/crave the Word, it is your covenant and all its promises are true. The Word is what returns to us accomplished, without it we don't have that promise. It's in Him that we live and move and have our being. Without the Word of God we are empty, powerless and without direction. We must make His Word our daily indulgence.

Right now in the name of Jesus I bind fear, anxiety, stress, sickness, hurt and any feeling of being overwhelmed; you won't be allowed access in this mind, heart or body. Jesus is the Owner and the Resident in this temple. I release miracle faith right now, that every thought, fiber and cell in your body is full of JESUS, His power and His light. I decree the Word of God that NO WEAPON - NO THING - NOTHING formed against you will prosper or can harm you, by ANY MEANS!!!!!

I release peace that passes ALL understanding and joy to flood over you.

Go forward with a smile, woman of God. You're covered by the blood of Jesus on the door posts of your life and surrounded by a host of mighty angels.

Force a smile on your face. God created your body so that when you smile it actually releases a happy chemical in your body.

SMILE.

Laughter is good, like medicine, so take a dose of medicine and laugh.

You choose what you put on, Wear JESUS!

You don't walk this road alone. You're not facing this battle alone. You are not alone.

"I know the LORD is always with me. I will not be shaken, for he is right beside me. No wonder my heart is glad, and I rejoice. My body rests in safety.
You will show me the way of life, granting me the joy of Your presence and the pleasures of living with You forever."Psalms 16:8-9, 11

He's holding your hand.
"For I hold you by your right hand— I, the Lord your God. And I say to you, 'Don't be afraid. I am here to help you." Isaiah 41:13

May He be your Prince of Peace, Wonderful Counselor & Mighty Savior. (Isaiah 9:6)

You won't slip and fall, He is holding your hand.
He's speaking counsel in your ear, holding your hand.
There is such peace in knowing that the ALMIGHTY KING is holding your hand. As you walk through this day take comfort in knowing who's holding your hand.

Day 28

Pray for your husband, build him up and speak encouragement to him. The enemy of your soul, of your marriage, would love to get you to think and speak negative of him. You overcome that with your testimony of his good.

If you're not filling your mind and mouth with good, building words, then the accuser is ready day and night to tear him down.

Overcome by the blood of the Lamb and the word of your testimony. PRAY AND SPEAK LIFE AND BLESSING.

If you've gotten caught in the enemy's trap, turn from negative thoughts and words and you'll strengthen your husband and your marriage.

"The accuser of our brethren, he who keeps bringing before our God charges against them day and night, has been cast out! And they have overcome (conquered) him by means of the blood of the Lamb and by the utterance of their testimony." Revelation 12:10-11

Be an example of a good wife and marriage, not only to the church, but also to the world. Remember how you treat your husband is how you are treating God.

Wives submit to your husband as unto God.
(Ephesians 5:22-24)

SEE what you are believing God for with your spiritual eyes, WRITE THE VISION, make it plain (put it where you can speak it and see it).
YOU WILL HAVE WHAT YOU HAVE BELIEVED!

It's time to dream again, believe big and exercise FAITH. Watch God do amazing things. Shake off the dust, get out of the rut and YOU WILL MAKE YOUR WAY PROSPEROUS, and then you will have good success. (Joshua 1:8)

"For assuredly, I say to you, whoever says to this mountain, 'Be removed and be cast into the sea,' and does not doubt in his heart, but believes that those things he says will be done, he will have whatever he says. Therefore I say to you, whatever things you ask when you pray, believe that you receive them, and you will have them." Mark 11:23-24

See what He has given you....
"SEE, I have SET (established, made firm) before you today life and good." Deuteronomy 30:15

Behold (SEE) I have given you authority...
Luke 10:19

Have confidence/trust that it WILL happen.

"Faith is the confidence that what we hope for will actually happen." Hebrews 11:1

"Then the LORD answered me and said: 'Write the vision and make it plain on tablets, that he may run who reads it. For the vision is yet for an appointed time; but at the end it will speak, and it will not lie. Though it tarries, wait for it; because it will surely come, it will not tarry.'"
Habakkuk 2:2-3

YOU WILL MAKE YOUR WAY...

If only we can realize that people who complain, criticize, quarrel, tear down and are negative, are actually hurting and IN SIN.

>>>>ITS TOXIC AND HIGHLY CONTAGIOUS<<<<

Good people, people you love, can fall into this. Stop giving it an ear, or any kind of sympathy. Most of all, certainly don't take offense by it. It'll take your light, passion and soul down with it. LOVE THEM, BUT DON'T JOIN THEM. Call it out for what it is and if you can't, *stay away from them and pray for them.*

He who loves strife and is quarrelsome loves sin and involves himself in guilt; he who raises high his gateway and is boastful and arrogant invites destruction. He who has a wayward and crooked mind finds no good, and he who has a willful and contrary tongue will fall into calamity. James 3:8.

A HAPPY HEART IS GOOD MEDICINE AND A CHEERFUL MIND WORKS HEALING, but a broken spirit dries up the bones. Proverbs 17:19, 20, 22

A good person produces good things from the treasury of a good heart, and an evil person produces evil things from the treasury of an evil heart. WHAT YOU SAY FLOWS FROM WHAT IS IN YOUR HEART. Luke 6:45

It is **not** a compliment to you if they are coming to you. Even worse is the fact that they would be comfortable dumping on you like that.

Finishing is better than starting. **Ecclesiastes 7:8**

"Better Is Closer Than Starting Over" and you'll never get to the better life if you keep having to start over in every area; so you might as well push through to better rather than start over.

Isaiah 43:18-19 "Forget the former things; do not dwell on the past. See, I am doing a new thing! Now it springs up; do you not perceive it? I am making a way in the desert and streams in the wasteland."

Philippians 3:12-14 "Not that I have already attained, or am already perfected; but I press on, that I may lay hold of that for which Christ Jesus has also laid hold of me. Brethren, I do not count myself to have apprehended; but one thing I do, forgetting those things which are behind and reaching forward to those things which are ahead, I press toward the goal for the prize of the upward call of God in Christ Jesus."

Jeremiah 29:11 "For I know the thoughts that I think toward you, saith the LORD, thoughts of peace, and not of evil, to give you an expected end."

Job 17:9 "The righteous keep moving forward, and those with clean hands become **stronger and stronger**."

If we keep starting over with the garden of our life rather than just getting out there and picking the stones and doing some work weeding, we will never get to the place of being able to enjoy the harvest. It's the enemy's ploy to keep us from enjoying life, to tell us to just keep starting over, because he knows we will never get to enjoy our harvest.

We are going to have to eventually pick rocks and pull weeds in every area; so we might as well just do it now with the garden we've already begun. DON'T QUIT!

Extra Encouragement, because God is the God of *"more than enough"*.

You may have had disappointments, let downs and maybe even crushing blows that brought you down, but what I do know is YOU WILL RISE UP OUT OF IT! When you get knocked down, you rise back up. You will *not be utterly cast down*, for the Lord grasps your hand in support and upholds you.
"For a righteous man falls seven times *and rises again*, but the wicked are overthrown by calamity." Proverbs 24:16
"Rejoice not against me, O my enemy! When I fall, *I shall arise*; when I sit in darkness, the Lord shall be a light to me." Micah 7:8
"Though he falls, *he shall not be utterly cast down*, for the Lord grasps his hand in support and upholds him." Psalm 37:24
"He shall deliver you in six troubles, Yes, in seven no evil shall touch you." Job 5:19

If you're down, it's your day to rise up. You will see it turn around. Isaiah 54, Ps 126, Ez 37:1-14, Mark 8:24-25, Ps 107:19-20, 2 Kings 6:16-17, Job 42:10-14, Rom 5:3-5

Suddenly there was a great earthquake, so that the foundations of the prison were shaken; and immediately all the doors were opened, and everyone's bonds were loosened. Acts 16:26
"**Suddenly**, there was a bright light in the cell, and an angel of the Lord stood before Peter. The angel struck him on the side to awaken him and said, "Quick! Get up!" And the chains fell off his wrists...They passed the first and second guard posts and came to the iron gate leading to the city, and this opened for them all by itself. So they passed through and started walking down the street, and then the angel suddenly left him." Acts 12:7, 10

God's going to turn it around, SUDDENLY. Get ready.
In faith and expectancy you need to enlarge your tent and
expand the length of your ropes. You might be down,
empty and dry but you WILL RISE UP.
Today's a new day, today's your day.
Look up, the answers are on the way.
Hope in God's suddenly miracle power that's proven
AGAIN AND AGAIN.
You are an OVERCOMER, you are NOT overcome.

Stay the Course
In the classic novel by Homer the Odyssey, there was a
mysterious Island where inhabitants of the island
possessed enchanting voices that distracted sailors from
their journey, imprisoning them forever. Odysseus put
wax in his crew's ears and ordered them to tie him
securely to the ship's mast to prevent him from being
lured away by their enchanting songs as they passed by
the island. Odysseus commanded them to stay true to
their course no matter what happened.
Sometimes we need to put wax in our ears, shut out the
voices that lure us away, fix/set our course and tie
ourselves to the mast!!!!
I'm not changing course NO MATTER WHAT.
Stay the Course

~Pastor Rhonda Spencer